Original title:
Between the Leaves

Copyright © 2025 Creative Arts Management OÜ
All rights reserved.

Author: Miriam Kensington
ISBN HARDBACK: 978-1-80581-844-1
ISBN PAPERBACK: 978-1-80581-371-2
ISBN EBOOK: 978-1-80581-844-1

## The Nursery of Ferns and Seeds

In a patch where greens collide,
Ferns and seeds all try to hide.
They chuckle low, a leafy spree,
Playing tag with bumblebees.

Petals gossip, roots conspire,
Twirling round a dandelion fire.
Tiny sprouts with dreams to soar,
Whispering hopes, they can't ignore.

## Cadence of the Verdant Lullaby

Swaying branches hum a tune,
Bouncing beats beneath the moon.
Worms with dances, quite absurd,
Wiggle-wiggle, not a word!

Rabbits hop and tumble round,
Chasing shadows on the ground.
Squirrels giggle, up they go,
Popping corn from high and low.

## Sunbeams and Silent Songs

Sunbeams tickle ferns in glee,
Singing soft, "Come dance with me!"
Bugs perform a wiggly show,
As flowers blush, they steal the glow.

Grasshoppers leap with flair and grace,
Racing leaves in a merry chase.
With gentle laughter, breezes play,
A leafy jest to end the day.

## Echoes of a Leafy Reverie

Leaves converse in whispered tones,
Mice in hats trade silly puns.
Twirly vines join in the fun,
A leafy dance has just begun!

The moon peeks through with cheeky light,
"Who's the best? I'm quite the sight!"
While fireflies flicker, all aglow,
The leafy crowd steals the show!

## The Poetry of Bark and Leaf

In the park, the squirrels play,
Chasing shadows, come what may.
A tree stands firm, it can't flee,
While birds gossip, full of glee.

The acorns drop like little bombs,
Causing chaos, little qualms.
The laughing breeze just can't be tamed,
For every branch, a story named.

Nuts and twigs are their delight,
Creating mischief, day and night.
Yet, when the rain begins to fall,
The dance turns into nature's brawl.

So next time you step outside,
Join those critters in the glide.
Laugh along with rustling noise,
In this forest, we are toys.

## Lullabies of the Woodland

When nighttime falls, the owls hoot,
A serenade, strange and cute.
The rustling leaves sing their tune,
Beneath the winking silver moon.

The raccoons gather, sharing snacks,
While fireflies light the shadowed tracks.
The branches sway in sleepy cheer,
"Come join our party, bring good beer!"

The snoring foxes take their beds,
While crickets hum like busy heads.
Each critter dreams of acorn pies,
In this land where laughter flies.

So hush now, listen to their songs,
Nature's choir where all belong.
Wrapped in whispers, dreams take flight,
Dancing in the cool, soft night.

## Dappled Sun and Whispered Tales

The sun peeks in with playful rays,
Through leafy curtains, bright displays.
While trusty ants in lines do march,
A tiny army on their arch.

A brave young leaf, so green and spry,
Recounts the tales of days gone by.
"Just yesterday, a cloud went boom,
It scattered rain like nature's broom!"

The grasshoppers jump with silly wit,
They take their bows, then show a split.
Every stitch of light sings sweet,
In this laughter, all life's a treat.

So find a spot, lay down your head,
Join woodland friends in tales long-spread.
With every giggle, let's unveil,
A world where joy will surely trail.

## The Realm of Sun-drenched Paths

In sunlit halls where shadows flaunt,
The mushrooms gather, full of jaunt.
A hedgehog rolls, all spines a-prick,
Inviting laughs, he's quite the trick!

On winding paths, the daisies sway,
"Let's dance," they shout, come what may.
The butterflies wear quirky hats,
While laughing loudly, chuckling brats.

A picnic spread of crumbs and cheer,
As silly songs fill up the air.
The snickering breeze holds all the sound,
In this realm where fun is found.

So take a plunge, abandon stress,
With woodland friends, life's nothing less.
Amid the leaves, a joyful spree,
In nature's arms, we're truly free.

## Threads of Life in the Underbrush

In the grass a worm does wiggle,
Saying jokes that make me giggle.
A ladybug in red so bright,
Thinks it's a rodeo tonight!

A squirrel's dance on branches high,
Pretends he's skilled, but oh, my, my!
With every leap, he swings and sways,
As acorns fall in silly ways!

A hedgehog rolls to greet a bee,
They argue who is cuter, me!
With prickles sharp and wings in flight,
They buzz and poke from morn till night.

And there's a frog who wears a hat,
Claims he's the fanciest of that!
He croaks a tune, a bass so deep,
While tigers chase their dreams in sleep.

## **Serenity in the Shaded Nook**

A rabbit sipping tea so fine,
Complains the cup is just divine.
With sugar lumps that bounce and roll,
He craves a pastry—what a goal!

A turtle joins, so slow and sweet,
Says 'I'm fashionably late, can't beat!'
With every crumb he grins and munches,
Dreams of daisies and carrot crunches!

The breeze arrives, all soft and quick,
Tickles their noses with a trick.
A dance of leaves begins anew,
As sunbeams play in shades of dew!

The laughter echoes, bright and clear,
In this cozy nook—hold dear!
They toast with tea and smiles so wide,
A whimsical world where dreams abide.

## Nature's Veiled Encounters

A sleepy owl in slumber's might,
Wakes up to join the morning light.
He fluffs his feathers, yawns and stares,
At dancing ants without a care.

A spider spins a tale so tall,
Of bug parties held in the fall.
"Bring your dancing shoes," he cries,
While flies just roll their tiny eyes.

A fox trots in with style and flair,
Dresses in leaves, without a care.
He trips and falls, oh what a sight,
The forest chuckles with delight!

With every rustle, each small sound,
Nature's quirks are truly found.
In every nook, a secret's shared,
A hidden laugh, the wild's declared.

## Whimsy Under the Boughs

A raccoon dons a mask for fun,
Stealing from bins, on the run!
He gives a wink and grins so wide,
A treasure map, a pirate's pride!

A chipmunk juggles acorns round,
Declares he's found the best in town.
But as he tosses, down they crash,
He squeaks in fear, a bit too brash!

A deer prances, quite out of tune,
While singing softly to the moon.
With every leap, she spins and twirls,
A ballerina with head of pearls!

The world beneath the trees does cheer,
For every silly creature here.
With laughter loud beneath the boughs,
Nature chuckles and takes a bow!

## Tangles of Light and Whisper

Sunlight dances, a playful tease,
A squirrel's acorn, rolled with ease.
Twisting shadows, the chatty breeze,
Nature giggles, if you listen, please.

The leaves gossip, in rustling tones,
Secrets shared with the little drones.
A butterfly flutters, in bright disco zones,
Nature's laughter, in hues and moans.

## **Silent Conversations of Branches**

Branches wave, in a nonsensical chat,
An owl listens, wearing a hat.
With leafy eyebrows, they gossip and spat,
About the critters that scamper and scat.

Twigs point fingers, oh what a scene,
As the breeze hums a tune, so serene.
A crow adds wit, sharp and mean,
And the trees giggle, feeling quite keen.

## The Hidden Heart of Forests

Beneath the canopy, a riddle unfolds,
A hedgehog snickers, with tales of old.
The roots entwined, like stories retold,
Every nook whispers, with laughter bold.

The mushrooms chuckle, in colors so bright,
They tell of the moon and dance in the night.
A rabbit nearby, with a curious bite,
Jumps in surprise, what a silly sight!

## Murmurs of Mossy Paths

Mossy cushions underfoot, oh so soft,
The trees sway gently, as if to loft.
A ladybug struts, feeling quite oft,
And a snail gives a wink, ever so scoffed.

Whispers of fauna, a playful round,
Each rustle and chatter, a humorous sound.
A fox hides, laughing, just out of bound,
As the leaves erupt, with joy unbound.

## Dance of the Dappled Sun

The sunbeams do a wiggle dance,
Tickling leaves with their bright prance.
Squirrels giggle, tease and twirl,
Chasing shadows in a whirl.

Breezes play a game of tag,
Whispering secrets, don't you brag!
A chipmunk wears a leafy hat,
While butterflies steal snacks from chat.

Dancing ants in tiny lines,
Waltzing on the grassy dines.
The whole place giggles, oh so loud,
Nature's joy creates a crowd.

Laughing trees sway side to side,
In this forest, fun won't hide.
Tickled leaves and silly sights,
A sunlit show that's pure delights.

## Beneath the Verdant Veil

Under green canopies we laugh,
Telling tales of a cheeky calf.
Frogs croak jokes, oh what a sound,
While rabbits hop and bounce around.

Worms in their jackets take a stroll,
Feeling quite dapper, oh so whole.
A breeze whispers, "Come and play,"
As mushrooms giggle their own way.

The sun peeks in with a teasing grin,
Chasing shadows, watch them spin.
A chasing game of light and shade,
Isn't this the best parade?

Underneath this leafy dome,
Everyone feels quite at home.
Nature's chuckles fill the space,
A jolly, vibrant, leafy place.

## Shadows of the Sunlit Grove

In the grove where sunlight plays,
Shadows dance in funny ways.
A critter winks, a leaf gives chase,
While laughter echoes all over the place.

A bird sings songs of clumsy flight,
Flapping wings with all their might.
A frog mistakenly jumps too high,
Splashing mud as he flops by.

The giggling roots tickle feet,
As nature's pals all take a seat.
The sun bestows its shining light,
Creating silliness, pure delight.

Join the fun in dappled shade,
With every laugh, a memory made.
The joyful whispers swirl and cheer,
In the grove where we have no fear.

# **Echoes from the Green Hush**

In a hush where echoes play,
Laughter bounces, brightens the day.
A squirrel attempts to dance a jig,
While a beetle rolls a tiny fig.

Leaves chuckle as the wind blows by,
Whispers of humor, oh my, oh my!
A fox struts, wearing a flower crown,
Its royal demeanor turns some frowns down.

Raindrops tap an upbeat tune,
While the daisies sway and swoon.
In this green world, no room for gloom,
Only fun in nature's bloom.

Echoes of joy, they softly swell,
In this vibrant, leafy shell.
So come, let's frolic, skip, and run,
Creating echoes of our fun!

## The Gentle Hand of Nature

A squirrel in a tiny hat,
Steals cookies from the picnic mat.
A rabbit wears some shades, you see,
Laughing loud with glee and glee.

The trees are whispering their plans,
While ants throw tiny dance-off jams.
With twigs as microphones on stage,
Nature holds its wild rampage.

The breeze pulls pranks that tickle cheeks,
The brook is giggling, so to speak.
With every rustle, life's a play,
In nature's crowd, we laugh away.

## **Serenity Found in Green Corners**

In grassy nooks, the frogs recite,
Poems that wiggle, quite a sight.
A ladybug breaks into a dance,
As butterflies join in the prance.

The flowers giggle with petals bright,
Chatting softly, what a delight.
With daisies cracking jokes all day,
Serenity, but make it play!

A hedgehog sports a little grin,
For every worm, they chase and spin.
Life is good with nature's cheer,
In corners green, joy's always near.

## Foraging for Sunlight Underneath

Beneath the boughs, there's a spread,
Of mushrooms wearing hats instead.
They barter for a spot in sun,
And giggle as they play, just fun!

The caterpillars picnic grand,
While grasshoppers lend a hand.
Sipping dew like fancy tea,
A lively bash, oh can't you see?

With shadows playing hide-and-seek,
The sunlight's shy, oh so unique.
A whimsical world, full of jest,
Foraging dreams is simply the best.

## Dreams Cradled in Leafy Shadows

In leafy shadows, dreams take flight,
While hedgehogs plan a wild night.
They talk of stars and moonlit quests,
With laughter bubbling in their chests.

A snail with shades glides on the ground,
While beetles form a funky sound.
They gather 'round to tell tall tales,
Of adventures beyond the trails.

The whispers weave a funny plot,
Of falling acorns, oh what a lot!
In nature's lap, with joy we bask,
In dreams that play, we don't need to ask.

## Elysium of Sunlit Glades

In a place where the sunlight glows,
Squirrels balance on tiny toes,
Chasing shadows, they dart and dive,
Their giggles make the fairies jive.

The grass tickles at my feet,
As bumblebees hum their sweet beat.
I trip on vines, do a little spin,
Nature's slapstick makes me grin.

Mushrooms wear hats, so very bold,
Telling secrets to the old,
A dance of ferns, a breeze so light,
Sunlit glades put me in flight.

Lying down, I dream of cheese,
As ants march on with no unease.
In this paradise where laughter stays,
I find joy in the sun's playful rays.

## Colors of Silence in the Thicket

In the thicket, where whispers roam,
Crickets rattle like a noisy phone.
A deer sneezes, causing quite a scene,
While berry bushes giggle, bright and green.

Rabbits hop, they play peek-a-boo,
With a chorus of frogs that croak, 'Who's who?'
Blushing flowers in vivid attire,
Hold a garden party in green attire.

Jays squawk their laughter up in the trees,
While butterflies flit with the utmost ease.
Can you hear the humor in the rustling leaves?
Nature's comedy, oh how it weaves!

I promise you, it's never a bore,
When a snail strolls in and checks the score.
In this thicket, colors play, it's clear,
Every little moment brings cheer and cheer!

## Unseen Spaces of Green Bliss

In unseen spaces where shadows dance,
Lies a hedgehog in a tiny trance.
He dreams of pies and a jolly feast,\nWhile squirrels plan for their nutty beast.

The wind tells tales, with a twist and shout,
Making tree branches twist about.
I trip on roots, let out a squeal,
As leaves chuckle at my clumsy zeal.

The grass has secrets, it bends and sways,
Unraveling laughs in the sun's warm rays.
An owl hoots a punchline, wise and sly,
While rabbits' laughter fills the sky.

In this joy that surrounds us, there's no hurry,
As daisies gossip, can't help but worry.
The unseen spaces, full of delight,
Make all our worries take flight and light.

## The Soulful Whisper of Chlorophyll

Chlorophyll whispers with a giggly tone,
In a world filled with green, I feel at home.
Leafy characters tell jokes so spry,
As I laugh aloud, the clouds drift by.

In the garden, things are never grim,
A dandelion's joke leaves me in a whim.
The tomatoes wear shades to block the light,
While the cucumbers plan for a dance tonight.

Bumblebees buzz with a rhythm so sweet,
While everyone's grooving to nature's beat.
A melody swirls in the air, so fine,
As I join in the fun, sipping on sunshine.

So come along, let's share a laugh,
Join the greens in their leafy gaffe.
In this soulful hush, where humor spills,
Life shines bright with chlorophyll thrills.

## Breezes that Paint the Sky

A gust of wind, a playful fright,
Jumps the clouds, such a funny sight.
Dancing through branches, swaying high,
Leaves giggle softly, flapping nigh.

Whispers of laughter in the air,
Nature's joke, float without a care.
Tickling the petals in a waltz,
Swirls of color, nobody faults.

Mischief lurks in every rustle,
Chasing butterflies, oh what a hustle!
Crickets chuckle, sharing tales,
While squirrels prank and the laughter sails.

Sunset drapes in hues so bright,
Drawing shadows that tease the night.
With every flap, there's joy to share,
A canvas painted with breezy flair.

## **A Sanctuary in Chasing Shadows**

In a nook where shadows play,
A thicket hides in a silly way.
Rabbits hop, and frogs do prance,
All are here for a dance-off chance.

Dandelions giggle with glee,
Waving hands like it's a jamboree.
Under the oaks, they plot and scheme,
To make each shadow a funny dream.

A cunning fox, in a hat so tall,
Trip over roots, oh what a fall!
Laughter echoes among the trees,
As every critter joins in with ease.

Embraced by nature, joy takes flight,
Chasing sunset into the night.
Frolicking shadows, what a delight,
Creating a stage for laughter's light.

## Traces of Dreams Among the Flora

In gardens stitched with vibrant hues,
A mix of scents that spark the muse.
Petals giggle, teasing the bees,
Nature's fun in the softest breeze.

Twirling dandelions, sweet and sly,
Challenge the wind to a playful fly.
Whimsical sprites, in a dewdrop gleam,
Dance like they're lost in a quirky dream.

Beneath the ferns in jest they plot,
To swaddle the night in a silly knot.
Chasing the stars on a breezy trail,
Their giggles twinkle, never pale.

As twilight weaves through leaves so bright,
Whispers of joy take airy flight.
Among the flora, dreams might seem,
To float away in a vibrant beam.

## The Hidden Symphony of Trees

Oh, the trees that sway and sing,
Whistling tunes of the spring.
Branches tap in a quirky beat,
While leaves join in, oh what a treat!

Frogs beat drums on a hollow log,
Crickets chirp in a playful fog.
A melody made of rustling green,
Nature's party, a lively scene.

Squirrels act as the capering band,
With acorns scattered, oh so grand.
Every note a delightful tease,
Creating laughter among the trees.

In this symphony of fun and cheer,
Every note rings out so clear.
Where nature's jesters play their part,
A hidden concert straight from the heart.

# Embraced by Nature's Veil

I tripped on roots while trying to dance,
The squirrels laughed, I had no chance.
A butterfly winked as it flew on by,
In a leafy world, oh my, oh my!

Frogs croaked out their tiny tunes,
While ants marched in their tiny loons.
I joined their fun with a clumsy hop,
But landed right in a muddy plop!

Sunbeams tickled the grassy ground,
Where playful shadows danced around.
A rabbit giggled, a quick retreat,
As I stole a snack, how sweet, how sweet!

Among the vines, we formed a crew,
With nature's laughter ringing true.
Who knew a stroll could bring such cheer?
I'll come back soon, the fun is here!

## Reflections of Life in Green

Under a tree with branches wide,
I watched a cat give the wind a ride.
The leaves whispered secrets to the ground,
While I searched for fun that could be found.

A snail zoomed past, or so it seemed,
With dreams of racing, it surely beamed.
I cheered it on with all my might,
As bugs giggled at our silly fight.

I found a hat that was once a nest,
Wore it proudly, I was blessed.
Mice threw a party, and I was in,
Dancing with flowers, where to begin?

In this wild world with laughter rife,
The funniest moments embrace our life.
I laughed with trees, their humor clean,
Oh, life is sweet in shades of green!

## Whispers of the Canopy

Up high where the branches play,
I heard the leaves gossip all day.
A crow cracked jokes, not very good,
While critters competed in fun neighborhood.

A raccoon wore a bandit mask,
Embracing folly was his task.
He swiped my snack with a clever grin,
And dashed off quickly, oh where to begin!

Sunbeams spilled like golden wine,
As birds made bubbles with seeds divine.
I tried to catch one, fell from my perch,
The laughter rose, my little search.

So here I stay, with nature's jest,
Among the trees, I feel more blessed.
These whispers high, a sweet encore,
In this green laughter, who could ask for more?

## In the Shade of Secrets

In gnarled roots where stories bloom,
I stumbled on a toad's costume room.
He croaked a tune, a fashion show,
In funky hats and boots, what a glow!

A shady squirrel shared its tale,
Of nutty escapades, oh what a trail!
He jumped and twirled, his pride intact,
His silly antics had quite the impact!

Beneath the boughs, we laid in shade,
Where laughing shadows turned our parade.
I tried to whisper a squirrelly joke,
But laughed so hard, none of it spoke!

Oh, the secrets held in nature's shade,
Where fun and folly are serenade.
With friends like these, I can't help but say,
Life's a comedy in its own sweet way!

## Whispers in the Canopy

A squirrel with a nut in hand,
Gives acorns to his friend so grand.
But when he stumbles on a branch,
They both engage in a clumsy dance.

The birds chirp gossip, oh so sly,
While butterflies just float on by.
A chipmunk sneezes, scatters seeds,
And laughter grows among the reeds.

The sun peeks through with a cheeky grin,
As shadows play and fun begins.
The trees lean in to hear the jest,
As woodland creatures join the fest.

So if you stroll beneath these trees,
Prepare for giggles with the breeze.
For nature's joke is quick and bright,
In this merry, leafy light.

## Shadows of the Rustling Green

A rabbit hops and trips in show,
His floppy ears flapping to and fro.
He stops to laugh, as friends nearby,
Join in the fun with an echoing sigh.

The hedgehog rolls on spiky ground,
While crickets chirp their merry sound.
"Did you hear what the owl said?"
They burst with laughter, almost turning red.

As shadows dance in dappled light,
The bushes shake, what a sight!
A crow misjudges a branch to sit,
With a flurry of feathers, he's not so lit!

In this green world, joy surrounds,
With friendly banter as laughter bounds.
Adventures spring from every nook,
Rustling secrets in storybook.

## Secrets Beneath the Boughs

A beetle boasts of his shining shell,
While the ants all giggle, casting a spell.
They plan a party beneath mum's tree,
With snacks of crumbs and sweet honey.

A caterpillar trips over a twig,
Sighs, "It's hard being so big!"
But blossoms smile in dazzling show,
Encouraging all to take it slow.

A wise old tortoise joins the toil,
Teaching funny dances on the soil.
With soft shell moves and little spins,
He shows them how the laughter wins.

From cozy nooks and shady spots,
The giggles echo, what fun they've got!
In every cranny of this wood,
The laughter spreads, all understood.

## Serenade of the Forest Floor

The mushrooms sing a silly tune,
While fireflies flicker, lighting the moon.
A mouse juggles crumbs, what a sight,
Balancing snacks through the joyful night.

A raccoon's eyes twinkle with delight,
As he dances around in the pale moonlight.
He trips over roots and makes a face,
With all his friends giggling in place.

The breeze whispers jokes from tree to tree,
And everyone bursts out in glee.
From every nook, a sound to hear,
A forest full of wit and cheer.

So wander down the winding trail,
Where laughter lingers, never stale.
In this serenade of night so bright,
The forest sings, "Come join the light!"

## **Veils of Flora and Fauna**

A wise old tree with eyes so wide,
Swears he saw a squirrel hide.
In a sock, or was it a shoe?
Nutty fashion, a sight to view!

The daisies giggle, the roses tease,
Whispering secrets in the breeze.
A sunflower struts in a funky hat,
Claiming he's the coolest plant, just like that!

A caterpillar with dance so grand,
Pulled off moves no one had planned.
Beetles joined in on the fun,
While ants got tired, no more to run!

So if you listen as you stroll,
You might just hear their little goal.
To make you smile, to make you laugh,
Nature's comedy, a quirky craft!

## When the Breeze Speaks in Hues

A breeze blew in on a sunny morn,
Making all flowers do a horned.
Petals flutter, a wild ballet,
Colorful chaos, come out to play!

The lilacs murmured in a twist,
"Pink is great, but purple? Don't miss!"
The daisies smiled with their white shoe laces,
Jumping up high, flipping our bases!

Then came a robin with a wink and tweet,
Who challenged a daffodil for a beat.
"Oh, try to catch me!" with a flapping show,
But all it caught was a sun-too-glow!

In this garden of cheeky tunes,
You'll find laughter 'neath the moons.
So next time you roam, give a cheeky cheer,
And let the colors brighten your sphere!

## Life Beyond the Bark

A wise old oak gave a hearty laugh,
As squirrels plotted heist of a snack.
"Stealing seeds? Oh my, so bold!
I hope you don't end up with mold!"

The woodpecker drummed a jazzy beat,
While rabbits danced on their tiny feet.
Life's too fun, forget the bark,
Let's celebrate all, from dawn till dark!

Vines swing like a rope in a show,
Covering mishaps, oh boy, what a blow!
Nature's circus, wild and free,
With an audience of bumblebees!

So gather around for a zany spree,
Where giggles bloom like flowers, you see.
In the woods where whimsy takes flight,
Every day's a comical delight!

## Harmonies Lost amongst the Arboreal

In a waltz of branches, a squirrel burst,
To sing a tune he thought was first.
But it turned out to be a thrush's grace,
Now they argue who holds the place!

Down below, the grasses sway,
Join the chorus that likes to play.
"Hey, no solos! This is a choir!"
In harmony's struggle, their bonds inspire!

The bushes chuckle, their leaves applaud,
As nature's jesters give a nod.
A snail in the back is taking a nap,
Missing the fun, all in a flap!

Yet among this ruckus and merry cheer,
Lies the truth that's very clear.
In the rustle and hum, so strangely divine,
All are welcome, each laugh's a sign!

## Journey Through the Quivering Branches

Wiggly worms dance on a twig,
Squirrel's acrobatics, do a jig,
A bird shouts orders, quite absurd,
In this wood, nonsense is the word.

A rabbit hops, gets stuck in a vine,
While ants hold court, sipping sweet brine,
The sun peeks in, to see the show,
Leaves giggle softly, 'Oh, what a blow!'

The breeze carries tales of cheeky theft,
As chipmunks argue over the left,
Nut-diner etiquette's all out of whack,
Amongst the banter, no one looks back.

High above, a crow makes a fuss,
Watching the chaos, just like us,
Nature's circus, with a daily cast,
In this green theatre, laughter is vast.

## Murmurs in the Shade

Whispers echo where sunbeams creep,
Lizards gossip while others sleep,
Moments of magic, silliness reigns,
In the grass, a royal porch the remains.

Frogs throw a party, a ribbit parade,
While crickets provide a serenade,
Sunflower hats on each tiny head,
Making sure that no one feels dread.

Breezes tickle the flowers so bright,
They dance and giggle, what a sight,
The roots below play tug of war,
In this dappled realm, you'll find much more.

Even the stones join in the fun,
Chatting 'bout leaves and the warm sun,
Here in the shade, joy's the main theme,
Nature's laughter flows like a sweet dream.

## The Language of the Understory

Mossy mats blanket the ground so knobby,
Fungi debate who's the biggest hobby,
Decomposers whisper, 'Let's share the cake!'
While worms groove, making no mistake.

Beetles high-five under rotting pine,
Rooted friends gossip, having a fine time,
The underground charades take flight,
Mud pies are served, what a silly sight!

Fallen leaves tell stories of yore,
As spiders spin webs to keep score,
Snails debate, who's taking the slow path,
In this green world, everyone laughs.

In the understory, laughter can't cease,
Each critter's giggle is nature's release,
"Join our folly," the mushrooms say,
In this leafy realm, we play all day.

## Beneath the Canopy's Embrace

Caterpillars strut with a swagger so grand,
In a leafy club where buddies all band,
Jokes fly like acorns on a fun spree,
Of what they'll become, just wait and see!

Around mighty trunks, the shadows play games,
Tagging each other with silly names,
Chipmunks oink, while raccoons all cheer,
Under the boughs, there's nothing to fear.

A dappled dance floor where fungi unite,
With mushrooms that twirl in pure delight,
The laughter bubbles up like a brook,
In this green haven, come take a look!

As twilight beckons with a giggly sigh,
Creatures of night prepare to fly high,
Wingtips and twirls, to the stars they race,
Under the canopy, joy's a warm place.

## Rustling Stories in the Breeze

A squirrel in a suit, quite absurd,
Chasing down a wayward bird.
Leaves giggle at their playful chase,
Nature's jesters, full of grace.

A breeze pulls pranks, whispers of fun,
Tickles the trees, makes them run.
Bark laughs as branches twist and sway,
What a party in the forest today!

An acorn hat, a leaf bow tie,
Critters gather, their spirits high.
Jokes shared under the sun's warm glow,
The woods are alive, putting on a show.

From rustling grass to a chirp or two,
The forest is a stage, a lively zoo.
Nature's humor, vibrant and free,
In the heart of the trees, joy is the key.

## Fragments of Nature's Canvas

Paint splashes of green, yellow, and red,
Foliage giggles, its colors widespread.
A beetle wearing glasses and a hat,
Struts through the woods, oh, imagine that!

Brushes made of soft, fluttering wings,
Creating a canvas, nature sings.
Trees pose for the painter's delight,
Each leaf a giggle, each branch a sight.

A fox with a crown, strutting in style,
Rabbits at court, they all share a smile.
Sunlight dapples in splotches so bright,
Nature's gallery bursts with delight.

Fragments of joy, a whimsical scene,
Every little laugh, a vibrant sheen.
In this forest, creation unfolds,
A canvas of life, where laughter is gold.

## Laughter of the Wind-kissed Foliage

The wind tells tales between the trees,
A stand-up show, intending to please.
Leaves dance around as if on a stage,
Cracking jokes, acting their age.

A chipmunk with dreams of a Broadway star,
Twirls and spins with a nut in a jar.
The breeze shakes its head, what a sight!
Nature's comedy—pure delight.

The rustle of leaves, a giggling crowd,
Whispers of love, playful and loud.
A rabbit hops in with a flourish and grin,
It's a frolicsome party—let the fun begin!

Breezy chuckles spill into the creek,
Washing the worries, making us peek.
With laughter as bright as the midday sun,
In this leafy realm, there's always fun!

## **Cradled in Nature's Embrace**

An owl with a hat, how charmingly absurd,
Hoots out puns that are purely unheard.
Squirrels take notes, forming a club,
In laughter's embrace, they all snug and rub.

The flowers chuckle, their colors a show,
Dancing in breezes; oh, what a flow!
A butterfly slips, laughing on the wing,
While petals erupt in a joyous spring.

The sun winks down, adding to the cheer,
Nature's embrace feels warm and clear.
In this gathering of fauna and flora,
Giggles abound, leaving us wanting more-a.

Cradled in joy, the world spins round,
Where whimsy and laughter forever abound.
In the arms of the wild, let your heart race,
Join in the fun, let joy interlace.

## Twilight Serenade in Leafy Tempest

In a rustling dance, the branches prance,
Squirrels spill secrets, in their nutty trance.
Crickets chirp tunes, they all sing along,
As shadows twirl in the twilight throng.

A raccoon with flair, wearing a crown,
Steals the last crumbs from a picnic town.
Oh, what a show beneath the moon's glow,
As fireflies waltz in the evening's flow.

### A Garden of Whispers and Dreams

Petals giggle softly, gossiping blooms,
While bumblebees dance in their fluffy costumes.
The daisies tease, with their cheerful grins,
While a dandelion sighs, dreaming of spins.

Worms tell tall tales, beneath the moist earth,
About summer storms and their valiant birth.
The wind joins the fun, with a playful nudge,
And leaves shimmy down, refusing to budge.

## Sounds of the Nature's Quilt

Nature hums sweetly, a quilt of delight,
With rustles and chuckles that dance through the night.
Leaves share the news of the ants' grand parade,
While frogs croak the gossip, their voices charade.

Woodpeckers tap to a quirky old beat,
As deer join the party on soft, padded feet.
They leap and they bound, with grace and with glee,
In this lively concert, wild and free.

## **Veins of Life in Nature's Palette**

The artist with leaves splashed colors around,
While butterflies fluttered, they twirled and they frowned.

Buds burst with laughter, each hue a bright tease,
While shadows painted sillies in the swirling breeze.

A painterly mess where the critters convene,
The flowers poke fun at the smudges they've seen.
With every brushstroke, they giggle and sway,
In this vibrant wild show, come dance and play!

## Echoes of a Woodland Breeze

In the woods, the squirrels chatter,
Leaves gossip 'bout the latest patter.
A rabbit hops with such great flair,
Wearing a hat made of dandelions' hair.

The owls hoot in a comical tune,
Dancing 'neath the chuckling moon.
With every gust, the stories weave,
A tapestry of tricks that won't deceive.

A chipmunk slips, oh what a sight,
Turns back and gives the tree a fright.
A rustle here, a giggle there,
Nature's joke is everywhere!

Through the branches, laughter flies,
A peek-a-boo from timid spies.
In this grove where mischief thrives,
Life's a punchline that always jives.

## **Tapestry of Sunlit Foliage**


Sunshine sneaks through the leafy screens,
Where beetles play kings and queens.
A ladybug holds court on a leaf,
While the grasshoppers dance without grief.

A butterfly trips on its own flutters,
As bumblebees share the juiciest mutters.
Green shadows hold secrets, so bright,
In this zany realm of pure delight.

Mice wear capes, they're on a spree,
Chasing down dreams as sweet as can be.
A toad croaks out a ribbity song,
In the woodlands, they all belong.

When sunlight winks, the fun will grow,
Nature's laughter is the best show.
All day long, the wildlife plays,
In this sunny realm, joy sprays.

## The Dance of the Old Oak

An old oak sways with a creaky cheer,
Telling secrets to all who near.
Its branches stretch like arms alive,
Inviting critters to jump and jive.

The raccoon drums on a hollowed trunk,
While a squirrel spins with a goofy thunk.
A woodpecker joins with a rhythmic knock,
Creating joy as they dance and mock.

With acorns bouncing in lively play,
The woodland crew makes a clattering display.
Grinning at shadows, they twirl and twist,
In this musical frolic, none are missed.

Laughter echoes from limb to root,
As woodland friends in laughter shoot.
Underneath the wise old oak,
Are stories and dances, a loving cloak.

**Veil of Verdant Dreams**

In the green realm where dreams don't cease,
Frogs wear goggles, as they leap with ease.
The bushes hold whispers of silly schemes,
Crafting plots in the light of beams.

A hedgehog rolls in a cloak of grass,
Winking at the moon as if to sass.
The snails slide in a synchronized race,
Laughing at each other's slow-paced face.

Under ferns where mischief dwells,
Bunnies share jokes that only time tells.
Silly shadows dance in the beams,
Painting the air in whimsical themes.

The leaves murmur with each little nudge,
Nature's jesters refuse to budge.
In this green veil, absurdities bloom,
Laughter echoes in the leafy gloom.

## Canopy of Hushed Wonders

Up high the squirrels chatter, oh what a sight,
With acorns bouncing, they take flight.
The branches sway like dancers in the night,
While birds sing notes that feel just right.

Insects hold their tiny court below,
Debating who gets the best show.
A wandering snail takes his time, you know,
Slow as molasses, he moves so slow.

The leaves, they rustle, a secret hum,
Whispering secrets that make us numb.
A tickle of breeze invites us to come,
Join in the chorus, oh what fun!

Nature's comedy, wild and free,
Unfolds in laughter under the tree.
With every giggle and silly spree,
Life's just a circus, wouldn't you agree?

## A Serenade to the Undergrowth

In shaded corners where critters lurk,
A frog on a lily does a funny perk.
He croaks a tune, his form a quirk,
Swiping at bugs as they go berserk.

The mushrooms gather for a wild rave,
Fungi groovin' like they're misbehaved.
With hats so tall, they look so brave,
And every dance is a risk they crave.

Ants march in line, a marching band,
Carrying crumbs, it's quite unplanned.
They've got a rhythm, it's really grand,
A tiny parade, oh how they stand!

Dandelions giggle, they play and sway,
Spreading their seeds, a fluffy ballet.
In this wild show, let's shout hooray,
For nature's humor, come out and play!

## Gentle Murmurs of Nature's Heart

Under the branches, the shadows dance,
A breeze flirts with leaves, a daring chance.
A rabbit hops by, caught in a glance,
With ears like sails, he's off in a prance.

The thistles giggle, a prickly joke,
While the daisies whisper, "Time to provoke!"
Sunbeams stretch out with a gentle poke,
Tickling the ferns as if to invoke.

A caterpillar plots in a leaf-lined nook,
Dreaming of wings, he's writing a book.
On this leafy stage, if you take a look,
You'll find that humor is nature's hook.

Oh, how the trees loom with grandiose flair,
With branches waving as if they care.
They laugh in the winds, floating through air,
In this leafy realm, joy's everywhere!

## The Maze of Leafy Kindred

In a maze of green, the critters play,
With hedgehogs giggling in their own ballet.
The trees hold secrets, each one a say,
What mischief is brewing at the end of the day?

A cluster of bees in a buzzing spree,
Dancing like pros, they hum with glee.
"Oh watch out!" cries a butterfly with a plea,
"I'm not a flower, please don't pick me!"

Twigs crackle underfoot like jokes gone wild,
Birds chuckle softly, nature's own child.
Frogs leap and croak, not at all mild,
In this vibrant show, we're all beguiled.

So wander through this leafy giggle space,
Find laughter in nature, a warm embrace.
Every rustling sound a light-hearted trace,
In this whimsical maze, joy leaves no place.

## The Stillness in Foliage Faces

In the shade, a squirrel prances,
Wearing acorns like fine trousers.
Leaves giggle at the silly sight,
As branches join in leafy fights.

A worm sneaks by with swagger bold,
Whispering secrets, tales retold.
Flowers chuckle at the show,
"Who knew trees could steal the glow?"

A beetle dons a tiny crown,
Strolling through his leafy town.
The crickets sing their nightly tune,
While owls hoot, "Come join the moon!"

Breezes dance with joy and cheer,
Tickling roots both far and near.
In this green, playful embrace,
Even shadows wear a smiley face.

## A Dance of Light Through Knotted Branches

Sunbeams swirl in leafy whirl,
Tickling fronds, making them twirl.
A shadow snickers, pulling pranks,
While sunlight winks at all the flanks.

A lizard does a quick ballet,
In this woodland cabaret.
Critters giggle with delight,
As twigs salute the dancing light.

Moths in tunics flutter by,
Whispering sass, oh my, oh my!
The leaves poke fun with rustling glee,
As nature hosts a jubilee.

Hopscotch games on sunny ground,
A dandelion spins around.
While shadows play their silly tricks,
In this forest, laughter sticks.

## Nature's Secret Fireflies

Glowing gems in the evening air,
Fireflies giggle without a care.
They waltz in circles, high and low,
Casting light in a cheeky show.

An ant jumps up, "Save me a spot!"
While crickets join in, singing hot.
"Let's start a rave!" the beetles call,
As stars blink shyly over all.

Ferns wave to the flashing crew,
As the night brings a colorful view.
A moth busts out in stylish flight,
"Who needs a crown? I own the night!"

In twinkling flickers, they weave their tales,
Echoes of laughter on sleepy trails.
The moon just chuckles in silver glow,
As nature puts on its best show.

## Fragments of Time Entwined

Rusty clocks hang from twisted vines,
Ticking slowly, sharing signs.
A ladybug with a tiny watch,
Says, "Hurry up — let's have a trot!"

Breezes carrying whispers near,
Leaves gossiping, oh dear, oh dear!
A pine tree leans with aged sighs,
"Time flies by like fluttering flies."

In each shadow, a giggle waits,
As the sun softly penetrates.
A mushroom shimmies, proud and spry,
"Who needs clocks? We just comply!"

With each tick, a shoot grows high,
While ants parade, just passing by.
Fragments laughing, lost in tune,
All wrapped up beneath the moon.

## Veiled Paths of the Woodlands

Squirrels dart, they play their games,
Chasing tails in woodland frames.
Mushrooms dance, a funky crew,
In their hats, they shoo and woo.

Oh, the owl wears glasses, so wise,
Peeking through with curious eyes.
The bushes giggle, rustling glee,
As rabbits hop, just wait and see.

The brook hums softly, sings a tune,
While frogs serenade the afternoon.
Ferns are flapping, oh what a sight,
A leafy rave, pure delight!

So wander down where laughter lives,
And nature's joy for everyone gives.
Under canopies, bright and soft,
The woodland's humor lifts us aloft.

## An Interlude in Greenery

Beneath the boughs, a picnic spreads,
With ants planning, in their heads.
Bunnies munching on carrots bright,
While the sun winks, pure delight.

A raccoon dons a chef's white hat,
Whipping up a feast, imagine that!
The pinecones roll in jest and cheer,
As ladybugs all disappear.

Napping turtles in a race,
Stumble over, what a case!
The vines twirl, thinking they're grand,
As petals break into a band.

So hear the whispers in the breeze,
Nature's laughs among the trees.
A lively dance of joy so pure,
In this green realm, we're all assured.

## **Tranquility Amongst Leafy Whispers**

The sun sneezes through a leafy veil,
As chipmunks giggle, tell a tale.
Trees wear shades, so cool and bright,
Watching critters in their flight.

A leaf fell down, quite out of steam,
Landed softly, slept like a dream.
Hummingbirds buzz with flair so bold,
Their tiny jokes, a joy unfold.

Sunbeams tickle the ferns below,
As dandelions sway to and fro.
The breeze whispers secrets ever sweet,
While the wildflowers dance on their feet.

So join the show, this nature's spree,
Where laughter blooms, and all is free.
With every moment, joyful we find,
The quirky woods, so well-defined.

## Shadows Caught in Twilight

In twilight's grasp, the shadows play,
Twisting branches, like ballet.
A fox finds humor in chasing light,
While fireflies blink, a curious sight.

The owls tease, with wisdom to share,
Hooting jokes, they lounge in the air.
Caterpillars giggle, doing their crawl,
While twinkling stars begin to call.

Crickets chirp, their band takes flight,
Riding rhythms into the night.
Moonbeams stutter, casting a glow,
As the woodlands whisper, ebb and flow.

So linger here where laughter spins,
Amidst the dusk, where joy begins.
The night reveals, under its quilt,
A tapestry of fun, perfectly built.

## Silent Stories of the Treetops

Squirrels in tuxedos, prancing around,
They gossip and giggle without making a sound.
Whispers of acorns, a banquet alight,
Wiggling their tails, oh what a sight!

A raccoon in glasses, recites a grand book,
While parakeets squawk, their own plot to cook.
The owls play charades, so clever and sly,
As they hoot out their secrets, oh my, oh my!

Breeze carries laughter, a tickle and tease,
While leaves do a jig, swaying with ease.
A penny for thoughts of the trees' silly dreams,
As they rustle and chuckle in sunlight's soft beams.

Together in mirth, they create such a scene,
Nature's own comedy, where all are serene.
In the heart of the woods, joy takes a flight,
Dancing on branches till day turns to night.

## The Space Where Light Does Play

Sunbeams peek in, like kids in a game,
Chasing shadows around, never quite tame.
Ants form a conga, just don't step on toes,
While light dips and dives, wherever it goes.

A squirrel slips down, it's a comical race,
With a fumble and tumble, it hides its bright face.
The sun giggles softly, painting the floor,
As dandelions sprout, wanting one more encore.

Grasshoppers hop, like dancers so spry,
Promising laughter underneath the blue sky.
A butterfly flutters, it really can't stay,
With all of these antics, it's restless today!

The trees lean in close, sharing their glee,
While sunlight keeps winking, just wait and you'll see.
In a world of pure joy, where shadows have fun,
Nature's bright theater shines bright as the sun.

## Harmonics of the Forest's Breath

Trees drum their roots, a rhythmic delight,
While branches snap fingers, keeping time just right.
The wind hums a tune, so catchy and spry,
As birds join the chorus, soaring up high.

Frogs croak in harmony, frogs in a band,
Each croak a note from a magical land.
Crickets strum strings, on each leaf they play,
A concert of nature, come hear what they say!

The sun echoes laughter through patterns of green,
As shadows sashay in a mischievous scene.
Every rustle and rumble forms melodies sweet,
In the symphony blooming beneath nature's seat.

Moss joins the chorus, in soft, gentle tones,
While squirrels add rhythm, on their little phones.
In this forest of folly, joy weaves its thread,
Creating a world where all fears are shed.

## Choreography of Dappled Sunlight

Sunlight performs on the forest's grand stage,
Dancing through branches, like a wise old sage.
Leaves play the tom-toms, so crisp and so bright,
As shadows do the cha-cha, under the light.

A chipmunk's twirl sends the ants in a spin,
While whirlwinds of petals give everyone grins.
The butterflies waltz with a flurry of grace,
In a ballet of colors, in this playful space.

The breeze joins the show, with a flick and a sway,
Encouraging laughter, inviting the play.
Each rustle a giggle, each flutter a cheer,
Nature's own party, come dance without fear!

With a twinkling of fireflies, night takes a bow,
As crickets applaud with a jubilant how.
In this joyful theater, forever we'll sway,
In a choreography where sunlight holds sway.

## In the Heart of the Thicket

In a tangle of branches, a squirrel did flip,
As a chatty bird offered a breakfast tip.
Beneath a bold berry, a rabbit went plop,
While ants threw a party, all wanting to hop.

A hedgehog in spectacles pondered his fate,
Over a snack that was slightly too late.
With laughter and giggles, the critters convened,
In this wild, noisy world where antics are dreamed.

The wise old owl feigned sleep in a tree,
While a raccoon painted faces with glee.
Under the moonlight, beneath buzzing stars,
Creatures kept dancing, forgetting their scars.

Each critter a comedian, rehearsing their plays,
In this leafy stage of whimsical ways.
Life in the thicket, a jolly parade,
With joys in the shadows, in sunlight, they played.

## Vignettes of the Wind's Caress

A gust whipped the hat from a fox's sly head,
He chased it in circles, oh what a dread!
The breeze played its tricks, teased a young hare,
Who tumbled in laughter, much less than a scare.

Leaves danced in patterns, a pirouette spree,
While a crow on a branch belted songs with glee.
A dragonfly twirled, a jubilant sprite,
Claiming the spotlight with colors so bright.

A tumbleweed rolled, thinking it's in charge,
While nearby, a porcupine tried to enlarge.
With quills laid out flat, he strutted with pride,
But the wind had other plans, gave him a ride.

As clouds whispered secrets, laughter took flight,
In the arms of the moment, everything's right.
With giggles and jiggles, all critters agree,
Nature's wild theater is where we are free.

## A Symphony of Fluttering Shadows

In the thickets, whispers of wings did collide,
With a chorus of chirps floating far with the tide.
A butterfly waltzed, in a skirt made of sun,
While a frog in the back did a leap for some fun.

The leaves cheered them on, rustling with glee,
A snail doubled as stagehand, as slow as can be.
Each creature played notes in this leafy ballet,
An orchestra thriving, come join the array.

A bumblebee buzzed, composing a tune,
Out of rhythm, yet joyful, beneath the full moon.
The dance floor was set, with moss as the rug,
And a turtle, quite shy, left his shell with a shrug.

With laughter and folly, the night was alive,
Each shadow a memory, quick to contrive.
In this swelling symphony, all hearts take flight,
As the world swirled around in pure, silly delight.

## Imagery of Nature's Canopy

A portrait of mischief hung high in the trees,
Where monkeys were plotting their next silly tease.
One tossed a banana; it missed by a mile,
Yet laughter erupted, extending the style.

The clever crow cawed, giving critiques,
While squirrels in pajamas enacted their peaks.
A chipmunk suggested a costume parade,
As nature drew close, in colors displayed.

The wind signed the score, with rustles that giggled,
While shy little fawns learned to dance and to wriggle.
An owl dressed in pearls surveyed the grand fun,
Join in, if you dare — it's a party to run!

In this canvas of chaos, each shadow has flair,
A tapestry woven with vivid, wild air.
With chuckles and cheer, all creatures believe,
In the magic of joy that they weave and conceive.

## Journey Amongst the Foliage

In the woods where squirrels play,
A raccoon dines on last night's stray.
With laughter echoing through each tree,
Who knew a mushroom could dance with glee?

The leaves all whisper silly jokes,
While ants parade in tiny cloaks.
A butterfly flutters, winks at a snail,
Unaware of the lemon in his pale.

A fox slides by with a cheeky grin,
Playing tag with a plump, mischievous chin.
Through tangled branches, they chase the breeze,
It's a party of critters, all buzzing with tease!

As I wander through this leafy dome,
I find my laughter, I've found a home.
Each rustling leaf sings a jolly tune,
Who knew nature held the best cartoon?

## Brushstrokes of the Changing Seasons

Autumn splashes red on every tree,
While pumpkins roll like they're feeling free.
A crow croaks jokes on a golden branch,
And two tired squirrels hold a dance!

Winter's freeze brings snowball fights,
As children giggle under twinkling lights.
A snowman grins with a carrot nose,
While a mime in mittens strikes a pose!

Spring erupts with flowers in bloom,
Daffodils strut while bees zoom and vroom.
A frog croaks tunes, jumps with delight,
Singing "Ribbit-rit, let's dance tonight!"

Summer shifts with parties and quests,
Where picnics gather the funniest guests.
A watermelon slice slips with a splash,
Turning laughter into a delightful crash!

## Festooned by Nature's Palette

In the park, colors come alive,
With kids and dogs, they run and jive.
A painter spills paint from a furry paw,
Creating a canvas that falls in awe.

The tulips giggle as they sway,
Trading secrets in a floral ballet.
While daisies throw hats to sunny glee,
They crown the passing bumblebee!

A sprightly gopher puts on a show,
He juggles acorns, oh what a pro!
With every drop, the audience roars,
For nature's jesters, there are no scores.

Under treetops, shadows play games,
As whispers tease and tickle names.
With laughter loud, we cheer and clap,
In a festooned world, nestled on a map!

## Footprints on a Leafy Path

With crunchy steps on a leaf-strewn way,
I stomp and giggle, come what may.
A friendly worm winks from his hole,
As nature's path reveals its role.

Each footprint tells of mischievous tricks,
From playful rain to breezy licks.
The chatter of crickets sets the score,
As frogs leap in for an encore!

A hedgehog hums a tuneful tune,
Bouncing around like a playful balloon.
The sunbeams dance, so warm and bold,
As stories of laughter are quietly told.

From squishy marsh to a prickly vine,
Every step's a jest, a twist divine.
So let's skip together, in joyful spree,
On this leafy road, just you and me!

## The Tapestry of Twirling Petals

In a flurry of blooms, the petals fly,
A dance of colors that wave goodbye.
Buzzing bees hum a silly tune,
While butterflies twirl like a manic cartoon.

The daisies giggle, the roses blush,
As squirrels pay tribute with a cheeky hush.
The wind whispers jokes that tickle the trees,
And laughter erupts in the rustling leaves.

With each gust of wind, the petals conspire,
They plot little pranks that never grow tired.
A jest from the lilacs, a quip from the thyme,
In the garden's grandstand, it's comedy time!

Yet in all of this mirth, don't be misled,
For the tulips tell tales of the dreams they've bred.
So come join the laughter in nature's grand play,
Where petals and whispers have something to say.

## **Secrets Suspended in Green**

Amidst the broad branches, secrets abound,
Where giggles of foliage can often be found.
A cat on a branch, with a sly little grin,
Claims to have seen all that goes on within.

The ferns are like friends, with gossip to share,
Whispering tales to the crows up in air.
The moss on the stone has a smile so sly,
Pulling pranks on the ants that march on by.

The sunlight winks through the leafy embrace,
Witty remarks of a graceless race.
And while the beetles compete for a prize,
Even the quiet will chuckle and rise.

So listen closely to the rustling show,
For trees have their humor, if you dare to know.
In jungles and thickets, laughter is green,
As secrets unfold in the spaces unseen.

## The Chorus of the Woodland

In the heart of the wood, there's a chorus so bright,
With owls on the mic, it's a marvelous sight.
Frogs croak the rhythm, the crickets keep time,
And the raccoons shimmy; now that's quite a crime.

The trees sway and nod, as if keeping beat,
While squirrels throw nuts like they're turning up heat.
The laughter of creatures rings out in the night,
As shadows join in on the melody light.

The badger, quite grumpy, insists he can sing,
But the owls just chuckle, "Come join the swing!"
With harmonies sweet that blend like a dream,
Even the mushrooms can't help but beam.

So gather 'round friends, where the wild spirits play,
In the woodland's grand chorus, we laugh and sway.
Each note an adventure, each laugh a delight,
The woodland's a stage for a magical night.

## Silhouettes of Forgotten Tales

In the twilight glow, shadows frolic and dance,
As echoes of stories give laughter a chance.
The lanterns of fireflies twinkle with glee,
Casting plots of old times 'neath the wise ancient tree.

A raccoon tips his hat, with a whimsical bow,
While the owls regale about their last row.
The whispers of brambles spin yarns from the past,
With punchlines that linger, and giggles that last.

Through silhouettes drawn on the canvas of night,
The shadows are sculptors, oh what a sight!
With each fleeting moment, new tales will unfold,
Twisted with humor, both daring and bold.

So come, join the whispers that swirl in the air,
Where laughter ignites in the cool evening fare.
These silhouettes dance, like a jest from the fates,
And stories keep morphing as night celebrates.

## The Embrace of Gnarled Roots

In twirl and wiggle, the roots do dance,
They trip on each other, like a clumsy romance.
A squirrel in a tutu, oh what a sight,
With acorns for jewels, it feels just right.

The old tree chuckles, a wise old sage,
As roots tell tales, in a leafy page.
"You think you're so clever," the bark does chime,
"But here in my shade, it's always snack time!"

A rabbit hops by, with a grin on its face,
It joins in the revel, a merry embrace.
The worms all laugh, in their underground beds,
As whispers of laughter float above their heads.

So next time you wander, look down with glee,
For the roots have a party, just come and see!
A gathering of mischief, wrapped in the earth,
In the embrace of gnarled roots, there's always mirth.

## Poetry of the Swaying Branches

Branches sway softly, on whimsical breeze,
They dance and they quirk like a clumsy tease.
A bird with a quill writes poems up high,
While leaves gossip gently, as clouds drift by.

The wind starts to giggle, tickling each twig,
As acorns join in with a playful jig.
The shadows stretch out, doing silly prances,
And sunlight joins in, twirling through chances.

Each gust is a tickle, a jest to enjoy,
Even the grumpy old tree gives a coy.
"A haiku or two may fall from my crown,
Just don't blame the gusts if they wear a frown!"

In this poetry realm, each rustle's a laugh,
Where branches become the jesters of the path.
So listen intently, feel joy in the air,
For in swaying branches, there's humor to spare.

## **Twilit Melodies in Starlit Canopies**

In twilight's soft grasp, the sound starts to hum,
Leaves whisper secrets, as crickets all strum.
A raccoon with flair starts to beat on a drum,
As owls lend their voices, oh what a fun!

The stars hold a concert, a dazzling show,
With fireflies dancing, all aglow.
The branches shake loose with a giggle or two,
While nighttime insists, "Let's have a brew!"

Mice join the chorus, with squeaks like a tune,
They dance on the grass illuminated by moon.
As shadows grow larger, the laughter grows loud,
In this magical night, we're the wildest crowd.

Yet the night's just a prankster, time slips away,
Reminding us gently that fun fades at day.
So twirl as you can 'neath the starlit display,
And laugh with the night till morning's ballet.

## An Overture of Petal and Leaf

Petals take to flight, a colorful spree,
In a somersault, they giggle carefree.
A butterfly winks with a flamboyant dash,
While ants roll a ball, a quirky little bash.

The leaves rustle jokes in a gentle tickle,
As frogs serenade with a fervent nickle.
One leaf claims a crown, a sillier boast,
While blossoms hold court, laughing the most.

Together they frolic in sunbeams so bright,
Crafting a symphony, pure delight.
An ode to the silliness fluttering free,
Where even the thorns know how to decree.

So sway to the cadence of nature's ballet,
With petals and leaves in whimsical play.
In this overture grand, humor won't cease,
For laughter is nature's most joyful release.

www.ingramcontent.com/pod-product-compliance
Lightning Source LLC
Chambersburg PA
CBHW070311120526
44590CB00017B/2631